Let's begin!

The application process might seem overwhelming right now, but don't stress. It actually breaks down pretty nicely, month by month.

This guide is here to help you stay on track throughout junior and senior year. It's not a flawless formula or an official rulebook. It's more like a lovingly crafted battle plan from a mom who's been through it a few times and thought, "Can someone just please tell me what to do and when?"

So here it is—a **month-by-month** plan. And keep an eye out for a few surprises and hidden messages along the way, including QR codes that share helpful tips and tricks to guide you through the process.

Write notes to
your future self

You did it!

JUNE

JUNE

Letters of recommendation

Getting a teacher recommendation for your college application is a crucial step in presenting a well-rounded and authentic portrait of yourself to admissions committees.

Choose a teacher who knows you well, share your aspirations, and provide them with pertinent details to craft a personalized and impactful letter.

Pro tip: Ask before summer break!
Teachers appreciate the early heads-up!

Senior Portraits

Book Now!

They are due in
early fall.

When you visit a college,
be sure to register your visit
because many schools
consider it a factor in the
application process.

TIP ALERT!!!!

Get on record! This is very important!

COLLEGES YOU'D LIKE TO VISIT
(THESE CAN BE VIRTUAL OR ONLINE)

COLLEGES YOU'D LIKE TO VISIT
(THESE CAN BE VIRTUAL OR ONLINE)

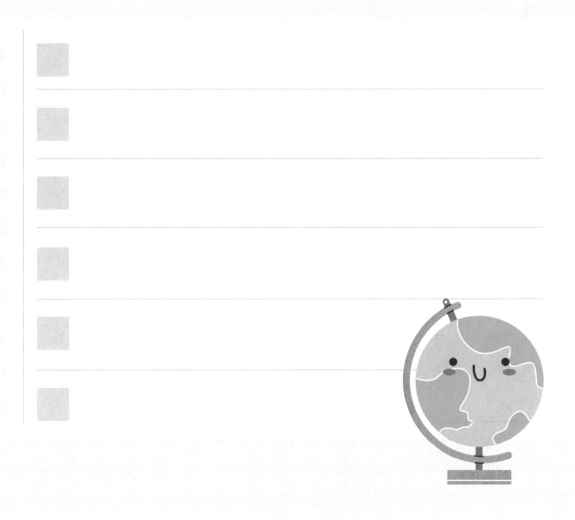

MORE COLLEGES YOU'D LIKE TO VISIT (THESE CAN BE VIRTUAL OR ONLINE)

MORE COLLEGES YOU'D LIKE TO VISIT (THESE CAN BE VIRTUAL OR ONLINE)

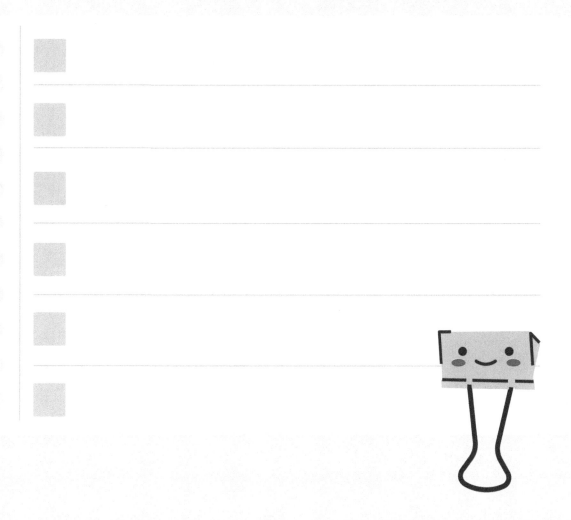

CREATE YOUR EMAIL ADDRESS

CREATE A DEDICATED EMAIL ADDRESS JUST FOR YOUR COLLEGE APPLICATIONS

Example: JSmithCollege2026@gmail.com

(Name + the word "College" + Year of graduation)

After you're in college, you won't want all the junk mail!

Important Websites

There are several key websites you'll use during the college application process to check test scores, compare colleges, and submit applications. Your guidance counselor will provide them.

On the next page, list the college websites your school suggests, along with your username and password for each (keep this info safe!).

USE THIS SPACE TO SAVE YOUR LOGIN INFO
(AND TRY NOT TO LEAVE THE BOOK IN THE
SCHOOL LOST-AND-FOUND).

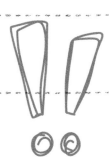

Attention Parents

Start a **group text** with a few parents of seniors graduating the same year, ones you feel comfortable with. The kind who won't judge if you miss an email, forget a deadline, or sign up for the wrong thing entirely. You'll have more questions, emotions 😊, and events than you can count, and a solid group chat can be a lifesaver. It takes a village to survive this!

Dream big
and
make it happen.

10 ACTIVITIES

In your college application, you'll have the chance to highlight up to ten activities that show what makes you unique and well-rounded.

Example List:

Internship at hospital	☐
Club rowing team	☐
Job at a restaurant	☐
Student Government	☐
Latin club	☐
Theatre	☐
Volleyball	☐
Volunteering	☐
National Honors Society	☐
Percussion	☐

10
ACTIVITIES

Enter your top 10 here to start. When you start entering your activities online into college applications, you'll be limited to just 150 characters per entry. That's about 2–3 short sentences **ONLY!**

Your List:

_____	☐
_____	☐
_____	☐
_____	☐
_____	☐
_____	☐
_____	☐
_____	☐
_____	☐
_____	☐

STANDARDIZED TESTING

Standardized tests like the **SAT** and **ACT** can play a huge role in the college application process, depending on the schools you're applying to. While some colleges still require test scores, many have adopted test-optional or test-flexible policies, meaning you can choose whether to submit them.

It's important to research each school's testing requirements early so you can **plan ahead.** If you decide to test, consider taking the PSAT for practice, then schedule your **SAT** or **ACT** with enough time to prepare through studying, classes, or tutoring.

June Checklist

- [ ] Request letters of recommendation
- [ ] Book your senior portraits
- [ ] Visit colleges virtually or in-person
- [ ] Create a college email address
- [ ] Get to know the application websites
- [ ] Organize your 10 activities
- [ ] Determine what you'll do for your standardized testing

JULY

INSIDER TIPS FROM RECENT APPLICANTS

Tips & Tricks

FLOWCODE

PRIVACY.FLOWCODE.COM

SCAN FOR TIPS & TRICKS

NOTE TO SELF

DON'T FORGET YOU ARE

- ☑ AMAZING
- ☑ BRAVE
- ☑ SMART
- ☑ CONFIDENT
- ☑ STRONG

College Essays

If you haven't started your college essays yet, now's the time. Aim to finish by the end of summer so you have time to reflect, revise, and get feedback.

Your essays are your chance to show who **YOU** are beyond grades and test scores. Let your personality, passions, and voice shine through!

Essay #1- Personal Statement

What is a Personal Essay?

Also called a personal statement, this is the main essay that goes to each college on your list.

Its purpose is to help admissions officers see who you are beyond grades and test scores.

Use it to showcase your personality, values, and what makes you uniquely you!

Research each college's requirements, including essays, portfolios, and test scores.

Start researching early so you know what each one requires, and **you'll be ready** when it's time to apply.

TIMELINE

YOUR MAIN PERSONAL ESSAY

Early July:
Use this time for self-reflection and brainstorming. Think about experiences, challenges, or moments that have shaped your identity, values, and goals. **What do you want colleges to know about you beyond your grades and test scores?**

WHAT IF YOU HAD A
CRYSTAL BALL TO SEE THE FUTURE?

Scan the QR code, then point your camera at the
crystal ball to see what it reveals...

Magical Reveal

FLOWCODE

PRIVACY.FLOWCODE.COM

SCAN THIS FIRST

THEN SCAN THIS

3DhappyAR™

Having Trouble? Go to www.3dhappyar.com/instructions

TIMELINE

YOUR MAIN PERSONAL ESSAY

Mid-July:
Start drafting your essays. Begin with a rough outline, then expand on your ideas. Don't worry about making it perfect; just focus on getting your thoughts down.

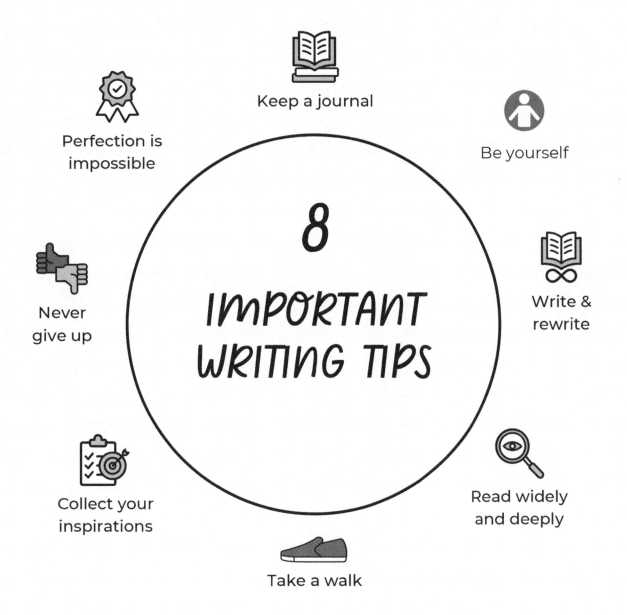

July Checklist

- ☐ Begin your personal statement essay

- ☐ Research each college's requirements (essays, portfolios, test scores)

- ☐ Continue working on your 10 activities

- ☐ Narrow down the colleges that you'd like to apply to and add them to the college apps

- ☐ Continue visiting colleges in person and online

AUGUST

AUGUST

TIMELINE

YOUR MAIN PERSONAL ESSAY

Early August:
Continue drafting and revising your essays. Start getting feedback from parents and peers.

Take their suggestions into account and make thoughtful revisions.

You're free to be different. Don't make it hard for you. Be yourself in the essays!

TIMELINE

YOUR MAIN PERSONAL ESSAY

Mid August:
Finalize your essay by checking grammar, spelling, and structure. Make sure it clearly reflects your personality, experiences, and goals.

Double-check that you're within word limits and following any specific instructions from each college.

Create a website to showcase your 10 activities.

Add your website to your application
to show photos of you in action.

CREATE A RÉSUMÉ

Showcase your unique skills, experiences, and accomplishments to help colleges, internship programs, or scholarship committees understand what makes you stand out.

Create a Linkedin Page

Creating a LinkedIn profile in high school helps you build a professional online presence, showcase your achievements, and connect with mentors and peers. It's a great way to track your accomplishments, support college and scholarship applications, and even open doors to internships or job opportunities.

Reminder:
Check in on your
letters

Recommendation Letters

If you haven't asked yet, now's the time!
And if you already have, don't forget to
send a polite follow-up email.

August Checklist

- [ ] Aim to complete your personal essay by the end of this month. Once school starts in September, senior year will get busy fast!

- [ ] Formally invite your teachers to write letters of recommendation.

- [ ] Begin creating a website, resume and Linkedin Page

- [ ] Review your college choices and narrow down your list to a manageable number of schools you plan to apply to. Be realistic!

SEPTEMBER

BACK TO SCHOOL

Welcome to your senior year!

Set up Interviews

Setting up an interview with a college representative or alum can be a valuable way to learn more about a school beyond what you see online.

01 **Receive Insightful Information**

02 **Gain Networking Opportunities**

03 **Stand out from other applications by showing your interest**

SIGN UP FOR COLLEGE FAIRS

College fairs are events where representatives from various colleges, universities, and educational institutions gather to provide information and interact with prospective students. These events offer an opportunity for students to learn about different educational options, ask questions, gather brochures, and get a better sense of what each institution has to offer. College fairs can be an essential part of the college search and application process.

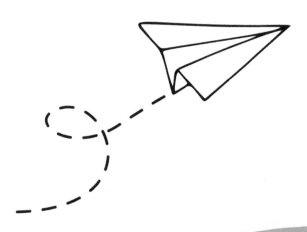

Early Action,
Early Decision & Regular Decision

The specific policies and deadlines for **Early Action**, **Early Decision**, and **Regular Decision** can vary from one college or university to another. Research and understand the admission policies of the schools you are interested in to determine which application process is most appropriate for your individual circumstances.

Early Action (EA)

Early Action is a non-binding application process. This means that if you apply **Early Action** to a school and are admitted, you are not obligated to attend that school and can still consider other offers of admission.

Typically, **Early Action** deadlines are in November, and applicants receive their admission decisions in December or January.

It allows students to get their admission decisions earlier, which can relieve some of the stress associated with the college application process.

It is a good option for students who are confident in their choice of colleges and want to demonstrate their interest in those schools.

Early Decision (ED)

Early Decision is a **BINDING** application process. If you apply **Early Decision** to a school and are admitted, you are obligated to attend that school and must withdraw any other college applications.

Early Decision deadlines are also usually in November, and applicants receive their decisions in December.

It is a good option for students who have a clear first-choice school and are willing to commit to attending that school if admitted. It can also sometimes improve your chances of admission at highly competitive colleges.

Regular Decision (RD)

Regular Decision is the standard application process with a later deadline, typically in January or February.

Applicants receive their admission decisions in the spring, usually around March or April.

Regular Decision applications are non-binding, and students can apply to multiple colleges simultaneously.

It is a good option for students who want to keep their options open and may not have a clear first-choice school or want to apply to a wider range of colleges.

TIMELINE

SUPLIMENTAL ESSAYS

September:
Once you upload your personal essay into your college application, be ready for supplemental essays to appear.

These often include questions about why you chose the school, your career goals, or even video responses. **They tend to pop up toward the end of the application process, so keep an eye out!** Count how many you need to write and see which ones you can repurpose for other colleges. **Find them now! There are more hidden down deep in those applications than you think!**

September Checklist

- ☐ **Finalize your college list**

- ☐ **Request transcripts from your school**

- ☐ **Double-check testing policies (test-optional, required, etc.)**

- ☐ **Ask recommenders to submit letters by October**

- ☐ **Meet with your guidance counselor to review your plan**

- ☐ **Set up Interviews at Colleges and with Alumni**

- ☐ **Polish and edit your essays**

OCTOBER

OCTOBER

Submit FASFA

FAFSA (Free Application for Federal Student Aid) is the form you'll need to fill out to apply for financial aid for college. This including grants, work-study, and federal loans. It opens every year in the fall, and the earlier you submit it, the better your chances at getting more aid. **Be prepared, there is a lot of information to gather and provide!**

NOW, SEND THOSE SCORES OFF PROUDLY!

Finalize and send your test scores
If your colleges require **SAT** or **ACT** scores (some don't!), make sure you've taken your final test and sent the scores to the schools that need them. Some colleges also accept **AP scores** for credit or placement, just be sure to check each school's policy.

APPLY FOR STATE
AND INSTITUTIONAL
SCHOLARSHIPS

Submit Early Action & Early Decision Applications (EA/ED)

If you're applying **Early Action** or **Early Decision**, make sure your applications are submitted by the college's early deadline, usually in October or November.

October Checklist

- ☐ **Submit Early Action/Early Decision applications**
- ☐ **Submit FAFSA**
- ☐ **Apply for state and institutional scholarships**
- ☐ **Finalize test scores and send to colleges (if needed)**

NOVEMBER

NOVEMBER

Continue to work on Regular Decision applications

Send thank you notes
to your recommenders

THANK YOU

THANK YOU!!!

Finish any remaining applications for rolling admission schools

November Checklist

- ☐ Complete applications for rolling admissions schools

- ☐ Continue working on Regular Decision essays

- ☐ Send thank-you notes to your recommenders

DECEMBER

YOU GOT THIS!

Finalize and submit all Regular Decision applications

Confirm transcripts and recommendations

Check in with your counselor to make sure
your transcripts and recommendation letters have
been sent to all the colleges you're applying to.

Baby
Photos

Gather your baby
photos for the year
book (awww!)

Keep moving forward, & you'll never have a reason to look back.

What is your quote for the year book?
Set aside time to research and write it.

December Checklist

- [ ] Finalize and submit all Regular Decision applications

- [ ] Follow up with your school to make sure transcripts and recommendations were sent

- [ ] Make time to gather baby photos and submit yearbook info

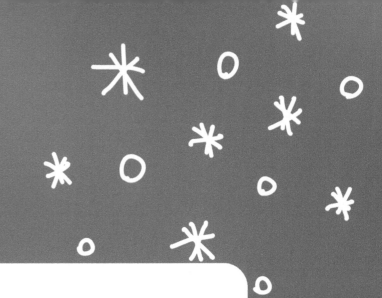

JANUARY

JANUARY

NEED A LITTLE LUCK? HOW ABOUT A FORTUNE COOKIE?

Scan the QR code, then point your camera
at the fortune cookie...

THEN SCAN THIS

Magical Reveal

FLOWCODE

PRIVACY.FLOWCODE.COM

SCAN THIS FIRST

3DhappyAR™

Having Trouble? Go to www.3dhappyar.com/instructions

Finalize and submit
any additional
Regular Decision
applications

REVIEW FINANCIAL AID PORTALS AND REQUIREMENTS

Private Scholarships

Ask your school counselor for a list of private scholarships you may qualify for. Apply to as many as you can! This is where your videos, website, résumé, and LinkedIn profile can really come in handy. **Show them who you are!**

January

- [ ] **Meet final Regular Decision deadlines**

- [ ] **Review financial aid portals and requirements**

- [ ] **Apply for private scholarships**

FEBRUARY

MONITOR FINANCIAL AID DOCUMENTS

KEEP CHECKING

YOUR EMAIL AND COLLEGE PORTALS

February

☐ **Monitor financial aid documents**

☐ **Keep checking your email and college portals**

MARCH

MARCH

Watch for Regular Decision results
(most come mid-late March)
Whoo hoo!

Review and compare financial aid offers

RSVP to admitted student events (in-person or virtual)

Each school has a different timeframe.
Keep an eye out and make sure to RSVP!

March

- ☐ **Watch for Regular Decision results (most come mid-late March)**

- ☐ **RSVP to admitted student events**

- ☐ **Review and compare financial aid offers**

APRIL

APRIL

Send thank you notes to everyone that helped you

(teachers, counselors, family, etc.)

THANK YOU!!!

Submit your deposit!

Let other colleges know you won't be attending

April

- [ ] Final college decision time!

- [ ] Submit your enrollment deposit by May 1

- [ ] Let other colleges know you won't be attending

- [ ] Thank everyone who helped you (teachers, counselors, family, etc.)

MAY

YAM

START PREPARING FOR HOUSING, ORIENTATION, AND YOUR COLLEGE ADVENTURE

Time to get ready for college life. Start by submitting your housing application, registering for orientation, and setting up your student accounts. Use this time to plan your move, explore campus life, and get excited for the adventure ahead!

May

- [ ] **Celebrate Decision Day!**

- [ ] **Start preparing for housing, orientation, and your college adventure**

- [ ] **You CRUSHED IT!**

YOU CRUSHED IT!

YOU TACKLED ESSAYS, DEADLINES, DECISIONS, AND
DOUBTS—AND CAME OUT STRONGER ON THE
OTHER SIDE.

WHEREVER YOU GO NEXT, GO WITH CONFIDENCE.

ENJOY YOUR SUMMER AND EMBRACE THE
ADVENTURE AHEAD, WHEREVER IT MAY TAKE YOU.